JUDY WAITE

KAI'S STORY

Illustrated by Chris Askham

BLOOMSBURY EDUCATION
AN IMPRINT OF BLOOMSBURY

LONDON OXFORD NEW YORK NEW DELHI SYDNEY

THE STREET

Lena, Kai, Sanjay and Chelsea live on Swatton High Street.

They are fourteen years old, and they are best friends. They'll never let each other down...

CONTENTS

Chapter One
The Fame Game

STREET-LEVEL

MAY BANK HOLIDAY EVENT

If you've got it - prove it!

Win the recording opportunity of a lifetime.

Sign up for auditions inside, or ask new owner Matthew Allsop for more details.

£20.00 per audition

Lena and her friend Kai were outside Street-Level, the local music place. "Look at this poster," said Lena. "Maybe I should enter? They might like me."

Kai looked up at the poster. "May Bank Holiday is only a few weeks away," he said.

Lena scanned the poster again. She was already doing a twirly sort of dance. "My old drama teacher used to say I had a good singing voice. This could be the break I've been dreaming of." Lena took her phone out of her jacket pocket. "I'm going to text Sanjay and Chelsea. We can go to my house. Then you can all help me decide what to sing."

Kai could imagine Lena on stage. With her blonde hair and cute smile, she'd be dazzling. "I'll write something original for you. Everyone else will do covers. You'll stand out if you sing something new."

Lena wrinkled her nose. "You're not a songwriter."

Kai grinned again. "I can try. My grandad was a musician, back in Jamaica. I've got music in my bones. Just give me thirty seconds to come up with something."

Kai clicked his fingers three times, then sang:

"I'm just a crazy boy with music in my bones,

I'm a sweet street-busker singing songs the
world don't know.

I'm a sweet street-busker, and I'll get you
through the night.

Listen to my song. Dance towards the light."

Lena stared at Kai. "That's brilliant. Sounds
a bit like Ritchie Ranx."

Kai laughed. Ritchie Ranx was his rapper
hero. It was cool that Lena thought he'd caught
that style.

Lena looked dreamy. "If I get a contract I might get famous. And rich. I'd travel the world. I'd live in a mansion. I'd get to know other famous singers and party with them." She giggled.

Kai had his own dreams. He'd get his dad a Porsche. Dad drove a taxi, and he only earned peanuts. There was no way he would ever afford a decent motor.

"Can I sing it, then?" asked Lena.

"What?" asked Kai.

"That song. I'd just change the boy to a girl, and get you to make it longer." Lena hummed the tune.

Kai shrugged. He couldn't actually remember what he'd sung. "Sure," he said. "But when you get famous, don't forget all your friends."

Lena hugged him, her eyes bright with tears. Kai wasn't sure if they were tears of joy about his song, or tears at the idea she might forget her friends, but he didn't really care. It was great having her as a mate.

He nudged her. "We'd better go to your house. You will need to practise. Text Sanjay and Chelsea and tell them to come. They can be your audience." Kai still wasn't thinking about the song. He was thinking about food. Lena lived near the kebab shop. He could grab a kebab for lunch.

Lena **was** thinking about the song. "I'm just a crazy girl, with music in my bones," she sang. An elderly couple smiled. A little girl started dancing. Lena blew kisses at them all. "I'm a sweet street-busker, singing songs the world don't know."

Kai clicked his fingers to the tune, then turned to see a teenage girl watching him. Not just watching – more staring. The sunlight touched her spiked red hair and it glowed gold. It looked like flames around her head. It felt weird to be stared at. Girls often looked at him, but not in a 'staring' way. Kai felt strange. She looked like trouble.

Suddenly the girl laughed. Kai laughed back. She was OK after all.

He felt good again. This street was a brilliant place to be.

Chapter Two
Sweet Street-Busker

Kai sat on the sofa in Sanjay's tiny front room, shovelling curry into his mouth.

Sanjay watched his friend slurp the meal they'd just begged from The Curry House kitchen downstairs. Sanjay's older brothers had both grumbled about Kai 'eating all the profits', but his mum had smiled. She had piled spicy chicken and rice onto a foil plate for him.

"Don't you get fed at home?" Sanjay teased.

"Yeah, but it's never enough," Kai grinned. "I'm a growing lad."

Sanjay picked Kai's phone up from the arm of the sofa and started filming Kai as he ate. "You can watch this later and be shamed into learning some manners," he laughed. "You're like an animal at feeding time."

Kai wiped his mouth with the back of his hand. "That kebab I had at lunchtime was ages ago. We spent hours at Lena's, watching her prance about singing."

Sanjay nodded. "Plus, the song sucks. It's got one of those pain-in-the-butt tunes that gets into your brain."

"Hey, have some respect." Kai finished the curry. "I spent all of thirty seconds composing that."

"It showed," said Sanjay and he carried on filming. "At least Lena sounds good. You'd be rubbish singing those words."

Kai jumped up. He grabbed the TV remote and held it like a microphone. "I'll show you I can sing my own song just as well as Lena," he said.

"Do it exactly like she does it," said Sanjay, laughing. "Give me some of that hip action."

Kai stood in the middle of the room. He pouted and wiggled his hips. "I'm a sweet street-busker and I'll get you through the night..."

Just then Sanjay's younger sister, Papri, came in. "What are you singing?" she asked.

"It's Kai's own song. Lena's going to perform it in an audition," said Sanjay.

Papri listened. "I like it." She sang along with Kai.

Kai swayed his hips. He flicked his hair.

Sanjay was still filming, and he held the phone up close to Kai's face.

"Listen to my song. Dance towards the light," sang Kai.

Sanjay kept on filming.

"I'm a sweet street–busker..." Kai stopped. He was laughing too much to keep singing.

"Let's get this stunning performance online," said Sanjay, grinning. "It'll crack everyone up."

"Everyone except Lena," Papri warned.

But Kai and Sanjay were too busy laughing as they watched the video. They didn't take any notice of her.

Chapter Three
Pressure and Promises

Kai was woken by the buzz of his phone.
It was Chelsea ringing him. "Hey Chelsea,"
muttered Kai. "It's Saturday morning and it's
not even seven o'clock. Is there an earthquake
or something?"

"There might be. For you, when Lena gets to you," said Chelsea.

"Why, what's up?" asked Kai.

"That video you and Sanjay posted online," replied Chelsea.

"What video? I haven't posted a video," Kai grunted.

"Check it out, quick. When Lena sees it she'll…"

There was a sudden hammering on Kai's bedroom door. "Kai? You awake? Lena's downstairs." Mum peered into the room. "You need to come down. She's upset."

"OK, coming. Hey, Chelsea. Got to go. The ground is already shaking," said Kai.

"Be careful of sudden sink–holes," said Chelsea. "And... be nice to her." Chelsea ended the call.

Kai sat up in bed, rubbing his eyes. He remembered the video thing now. He and Sanjay had uploaded his version of 'Sweet Street–Busker'. Then he had made his way back along the street to his own home. Why was Lena hassling him about it? He got up, put on his towelling robe and ran downstairs.

As he reached the hall, Mum was taking Lena into the kitchen. Lena stopped when she saw him. Her eyes were red and puffy. "How could you do it?" she asked.

Kai opened his arms. "We were just messing about."

"What's he done, honey?" Kai's mum put the kettle on to boil, then sat down to feed his baby sister, Marci-Lee. Marci-Lee was grizzling in her high chair.

"He stole my song. I'd rehearsed it for the audition." Lena's eyes welled with tears again.

"Did you do that, Kai?" asked Kai's mum. She turned towards Lena. "Don't worry. He'll sort it, honey. Won't you, Kai?" His mum made cooing noises at Marci-Lee. She got up to put bread in the toaster.

"Yeah." Kai's gut was rumbling.

"Promise?" sniffed Lena.

Kai hesitated. It was hard to think straight on an empty stomach. Why was Lena making a drama about nothing? What was wrong with posting a funny video clip online?

"Look, I have to go," said Lena, giving him a long look. "I'm working in the café this morning. But text me later. OK?"

"OK," Kai muttered.

Marci-Lee's grizzling got louder. Kai's twelve-year-old brother, Toby, burst into the kitchen. "I neeeeeed food," he said.

Mum rolled her eyes. "There's bacon in the fridge. Do some extra for Dad. He drove someone to the airport and should be back soon."

Kai needed food too. He was so hungry he could have even eaten the gloop Mum was feeding Marci-Lee. He headed towards the fridge, but Mum wagged a finger at him. "You sort that promise out for your friend, before you sort your stomach out," she said.

Marci-Lee banged her spoon on her tray, and blew him a food-bubble.

Toby grabbed a piece of fresh toast and tore it in half.

Bacon sizzled in the pan.

Kai groaned. "That smell. It's heaven. And torture."

Mum wagged her finger again. "Go. Now. Lena and her family are our next-door neighbours. We all have to look out for each other."

Kai groaned even louder. "None of you cares if I die of starvation."

He slouched off. Mum had said he had to keep his promise to Lena, but the truth was, he hadn't promised anything. And he wasn't sure that he wanted to.

Chapter Four
Going Viral

Kai checked his phone. There was a message from someone he'd never heard of, sent at 7.05 am:

@dantheman

Found your 'Sweet Street–Busker' video. Hilarious. I posted it to more people. It's got about 300 more views – just in four hours. Cool!

Kai opened the video link. The numbers viewing 'Sweet Street-Busker' had jumped up since @dantheman had messaged him: hundreds of strangers had rushed to look at him jumping about in Sanjay's front room. He had over five hundred 'likes'. Two more clocked up just while he was staring at the screen. "Crazy," Kai muttered, but he grinned. He felt good.

He watched the video. Sanjay had done a decent job. He looked at himself pouting, and the butt-wiggling still made him smile. Lena needed to back off. It wasn't as if he was going against her in the audition.

He scrolled down to the comments. Mostly from girls. There were eighty-three.

A cute looking girl called Dollface21 said his voice was like "liquid gold". Another girl, Jessiebaby, responded with "he's ALL gold".

A third girl, Prettykitty16, just put:

 Prrrrrrrrrrrrr!!!

"Awesome," Kai thought as he kept scrolling. "I'm collecting comments like a bee collecting honey." He laughed out loud. "I am buzzing. BUZZING. Bzzzzzzz."

A couple of guys had commented too.

One was a journalist, journo-jon. "Message me," he said. "This could be BIG."

His video was getting loads of attention. It was going to go viral.

Kai stopped laughing. Going viral meant serious money. And serious money was no laughing matter.

Chapter Five
Heart to Heart

"Can't you just take it down?" Chelsea asked.

Kai sat with her in the private garden of The Crown – the pub along the street that Chelsea's mum ran. Chelsea had an older brother, Tommy, but he was away in the army. Chelsea seemed to have got even more sensible since he'd gone. Kai had been hoping she'd calm Lena down for him, but the conversation wasn't going that way.

"Right, you two, toasted cheese sandwiches and hot chocolate," said Chelsea's mum as she came out with food and mugs on a tray.

"Awesome, thanks." Kai grinned at her. "I didn't get to have breakfast. I'm weak with hunger. I might just swallow the toasties whole."

"Lena's gutted," Chelsea went on, as her mum hurried back into the pub. "She thinks no one will take her version seriously now. She can't sing it in the audition."

Kai glugged back his hot chocolate. "She could sing something else," he suggested.

"She wrote 'Sweet Street-Busker' on the entry form. She'll have to pay again if she sings something different. And she says that was her song. You wrote it for her."

Kai felt annoyed. He hadn't written it for Lena. He hadn't written it at all. He'd just sung it, and then messed around with his own words. His **own** words! Why didn't Lena and Chelsea get that? "I'll pay," he said suddenly.

"Pay what?" Chelsea picked at a bit of crust, then flicked it to the ground. Two pigeons strutted close to where they were sitting.

"Pay for Lena to do a new song. If that's the issue," said Kai.

"It's not the whole issue," Chelsea was looking at him with her serious grey eyes. 'Sweet Street–Busker' is an original song. That makes it special."

"If it's that special, then it **should** belong to me." Kai reached for another toastie. "So, what do you think I should do?"

Chelsea bit into her own toastie. "You've got to do the right thing."

"What does that mean?" asked Kai.

"Follow your heart," said Chelsea.

Kai dropped his toastie back onto the plate. "You're trying to make me feel bad," he muttered. Chelsea wasn't being fair. Follow your heart. There was no way Lena would give up a big break for him.

He stood up quickly, scaring the pigeons away.

"Where are you going?" Chelsea frowned.

Kai shrugged. "My heart just went off without me, so I'm following it. Just like you said I should."

He walked away.

Chapter Six
Pretty Kitty

Kai sat on the bench in the park, watching children chase each other round the swings. His head was going round too.

He checked his phone.

There had been more comments coming in, mostly from girls. Plus eleven hundred 'views' and almost six hundred 'likes'. He had read that internet success was all about advertising. If he got enough comments then people would want to run ads on his video. But Mum would be angry if he didn't sort things out with Lena. All this pressure was doing his head in.

A shadow fell over him. He knew, without looking up, that it was Lena.

"Hi, Mr Popular – shove over." She wriggled next to him.

Kai moved over on the bench. Lena's puppy, Robbie, began chasing pigeons.

"I saw Chelsea just now," said Lena. "She said you got cross with her."

Kai shrugged. "Sort of."

"Because of me?" asked Lena.

Kai shrugged again. "Is everything always about you?" he said. He knew he sounded harsh, but why couldn't she see this could be massive break for him? He wasn't being out of order. It **was** his song.

"Is that what you think of me? Attention-seeking and a pain in the butt?" Lena was looking at him. The warm weather had brought out a new sprinkling of freckles across her nose and cheeks. She had the sort of eyelashes that were long and curled.

He sighed, and put his arm around her. "No, hun. That's not what I think. You're gorgeous. You don't need my stupid song to make you famous. You'll make it anyway."

Kai didn't want to add that this viral thing was his only chance, because it wasn't true.

He did OK at school. He was doing better than OK with his kickboxing. He had loads of options for the future. Maybe none of this was worth fighting over.

Lena smiled. "So you still love me? In a 'friend' way."

"I still love you. In a 'friend' way," said Kai, smiling back at her.

Kai waited for her to say the next thing. To start begging him to take down the video. Right then, if she had asked, he would have said 'yes'.

But she didn't ask. Instead she said, "I'd do it too."

"Do what?" asked Kai.

"What you're doing. Seizing the moment, of course," said Lena.

Kai frowned. "You would?"

"I've been thinking about it all morning. I've just been a drama-queen, but I was upset firstly about the music and secondly..."

"Secondly, what?" said Kai.

Her eyes glistened and he thought she was going to cry again. "... you made fun of me. All the pouting and hair flicking. I saw myself in a certain way when I watched that video, and it was horrible. I didn't even know if you liked me."

"Hey, come on," said Kai.

"No, I want to finish," said Lena. "I want to tell you that you must get everything you can out of this chance. I'm lucky to have you as a mate. I couldn't bear it if anything came between us."

"I won't let it." Kai put his arm around her and hugged her again, but his mind was racing. Now she was OK with it, he could reply to journo-jon.

He checked his phone.

There were no more journo-jon comments, but loads from cute girls. "Check these out," he handed the phone to Lena.

"Awesome. There are hundreds. What you need now is someone famous to support you. That's what makes things get massive. But…"

"But what?" asked Kai.

"All these girls. I'm a bit jealous," said Lena.

"Don't be. They might not be real. They could be fifty-year-old guys with bald heads."

"Lucky you!" said Lena as she kept scanning the comments.

Kai looked back across the park towards the swings. The children had gone, and there was just one person there. Kai frowned.
No wonder the children had run off. It was Archie Jenkins. Ginger hair. Pale skin. Thin as a stick-insect.

He was four years older than Kai, but Kai remembered he'd been kicked out of school before his final exams. Archie was bad news. Not just him either. His whole family seemed to have backhand deals going on in just about everything. They controlled people in the area. They messed with people's lives if anyone upset them. Dad said it was safest just to keep away.

Archie lit a cigarette. He kept checking his phone. As Kai watched, Archie looked up. He was a distance away, but Kai could still feel the burn of his eyes.

"Look at this one…" Lena nudged Kai, and he turned away from Archie. She held the phone up for him to see.

Prettykitty16: 🐱 you look prrrrrrrrfect

"I can't believe **that's** a fifty-year-old bald guy," Lena grinned.

Kai took the phone off her. "Hard to tell when she's got a cartoon cat for her profile pic."

Robbie bounded over, dropping a stick for Lena to throw.

Kai glanced towards Archie. He'd gone back to checking his phone, which was a good thing. Kai hadn't liked being looked at by Archie Jenkins.

Chapter Seven
Message Me

Kai sat in his room.

"How many 'views' you got now?" Toby stood in the doorway. Mum wouldn't let him have his own phone yet. She said he could look at the internet on the family computer, where she could keep an eye on him.

Kai looked at the numbers. "More than eleven hundred."

"Eleven hundred?" Toby whooped, then added, "Is that a lot?"

Kai shrugged. "Nah. Not really. Seems everyone's losing interest." He was trying not to feel gutted. He was also trying not to feel angry with Lena again. He'd gone to see Sanjay when he left the park, and they'd looked up the whole 'viral' thing.

It seemed you had to act fast for those fifteen minutes of fame. If he'd got on it that morning, when the comments were new, he could have kept it all buzzing. "There was a journalist guy, but I can't find him now."

The endless cute girls were still there, but journo-jon had disappeared.

Kai stared moodily at his phone, willing new comments to pop up.

"Maybe Sanjay could film you doing something else," Toby said.

"Doesn't work like that," said Kai. "I don't think you get to choose what goes viral. It's just got to happen on its own."

Toby thought for a moment. "Cats do well."

"What at?" said Kai.

"Viral stuff on the internet. Maybe Sanjay could film you singing to a kitten?"

"Yeah. Right. Helpful," said Kai. He rolled his eyes.

Toby was already backing out of the room. Kai could see he was bored. Kai had missed his one glittering moment when he could have changed his brother's life. His own life. His whole family's lives. He could have got rich.

It was early evening and he ought to go out, but he didn't want to risk seeing Lena. He'd been right when he said it was always all about her. It had been about her that morning, when she flipped out in his kitchen. It had been about her again in the park, when she decided to let him chase the dream after all. He glanced at his phone again.

A new comment. More than a comment, a message – and it involved a kitten. Sort of.

Prettykitty16: 🐱 Hey Kai, how are you doing?

Kai replied:

Kool4Kai: Surviving. You?

Prettykitty16: 🐱 You don't sound good for a boy who's just about it make it massive.

Kool4Kai: I wish...

And suddenly Kai was messaging her about everything. The buzz of the morning. The dreams for his family. How he'd missed his moment.

There was a long gap before she replied to his last message, and he thought perhaps he'd scared her off. Perhaps now the dream wasn't happening, she'd lost interest.

Then a message pinged back.

Prettykitty16: 🐱 You might find this weird, but I think I know you. In real life, I mean.

Kool4Kai: How?

Prettykitty16: 🐱 You live in East Swatton? Somewhere near that Street–Level music place?

Kool4Kai: Yeah. On that same street.

Prettykitty16: 🐱 I'm really close to there right now. Awesome!

Kool4Kai: That's unreal!

Prettykitty16: 🐱 We could meet up. I know someone who deals with music. You could still be massive. 😊

Kai was buzzing again. Prettykitty16 was somewhere near. She wanted to meet him. She knew someone who could turn things around. This was a cute girl who cared enough to try, and Kai wasn't going to waste any more chances.

Chapter Eight
The Waiting Game

Street-Level had just been done up. The new owner, Matthew Allsop, was building a new recording studio out the back but it wasn't ready yet. Instead, he was letting musicians practise and record in a long wooden shed.

It was going to be pulled down soon. Kitty's message had told Kai to wait for her in the yard outside.

A van drove in through the yard gateway. Four guys started to unload their gear. A drum kit. Guitars. Amps. Kai watched them as they disappeared through the back door into Street-Level. He would bet they had endless cute girls hanging round them. He checked his phone, wondering where Kitty had got to.

She had said this 'someone' she knew had booked the shed. They could work on his video.

This 'someone' would make sure the right people saw it. Kai thought about that Porsche again. The one he'd buy for Dad. He'd pay for holidays for the whole family. Maybe he'd even buy a house in Jamaica, and they'd spend their summers there.

"All right, mate?" said a voice.

The voice jolted Kai out of his daydreams. Someone was coming out of Street-Level. Kai stared at the pale teenager with ginger hair. "Archie Jenkins?"

"You got it in one." Archie lit a cigarette, looking Kai up and down as if he might be a car he was thinking of buying.

"Shall we go in?" Archie dragged on his cigarette, his eyes narrowing.

Kai shook his head. "I'm not here to see the band."

"Nor me." Archie took another drag. "I'm here for you. To talk business."

"I'm meeting a girl. Kitty," said Kai.

Archie laughed, a short burst of sound, like a gun firing. "Yeah, I know. She's already here." Archie pointed towards the shed. "Look."

A girl stood watching from the shed doorway. Not just watching – staring. She had spiked hair. Red. Like flames. "Hi Kai," she called. "I'm Kitty."

"You?" Kai frowned. "I saw you yesterday."

"Meet my half-sister. She's just moved here to live with us," said Archie.

Kitty stepped towards Kai. "Great to see you again." Her voice was kitten-soft.

Kai let her lead him into the shed. It would be OK if she was there. He'd met her before, sort of. He'd trusted her with his secret dreams. She wouldn't let anything bad happen to him.

Chapter Nine
Tech-Queen

"There's nothing in here." Kai looked around the murky shed. There weren't even any windows. "I thought there'd be a mixing desk. Lights. A mic. Stuff like that."

"I've got my laptop on the table along the back there. It's all we need," said Kitty, and she led Kai over to it.

Without the glow from the laptop, the shed would have been pitch black.

"Bands bring their own gear." Archie shut the door. "Matthew lets anyone book the space. He often leaves a key in the lock. He did that for me, this evening. He knew he'd be busy with the band."

Kitty tapped the keyboard. "We'll watch your video again."

Kai shook his head. "This isn't what I came here for."

"You came for success. A new future."
Archie said. "We can do that."

"How?" asked Kai.

Archie walked over to them. "Kitty, you're
the tech-queen. Explain."

And Kitty explained. It would be easy, she
said. No risk to Kai. He just had to set up a
new online account to run the video from.
"We need your name on the account and
everything. The internet people check stuff like
that. It has to look legit, or it will get taken
down, and we might even get done for fraud.
But as long as the original links are traced
to you then it'll be OK. But the truth is, we'll
control it all for you. Think of us as being

behind the scenes. Pulling the strings for you."

Kai frowned. "That makes me sound like a puppet. Why do you want this secret control? What will you actually be doing?"

"We'll be getting you all the 'views' you need." Archie smiled, but his eyes had that burn in them again.

Kitty squinted at the screen. "Your video massed a ton of 'views' but you need more. You need to get the internet traffic flowing." Kitty hit 'ENTER'. "I've developed some software. I can make up 'views' and put them against your video."

"How will that help?" asked Kai.

"When you get more than five million 'views' in under three days, advertisers get interested," said Kitty.

Kai thought about his eleven hundred views. They suddenly seemed pathetic.

"We can get big names to support you, too. Ritchie Ranx, for instance. You told me earlier he was your hero."

Kai thought about being linked to Ritchie Ranx. Awesome! "What's in it for you?" he said suddenly.

"We'll be your agents." Kitty pointed at the screen. Kai was singing 'Sweet Street-Busker'. The video still had only eleven hundred and thirty 'views'. "We get a cut of everything you earn."

"Trust us." Archie's voice was suddenly as soft as Kitty's. "We'll all get rich."

Kai frowned again. "Is it legal to make up 'views'?"

Archie laughed. That gunshot sound.

Kitty had her soft voice again. "Even the big companies fake their figures."

Kai imagined himself handing Dad the keys to a Porsche. Then he imagined Mum crying as the police dragged him away. "I'm not sure..."

"We got sent the link to your video from an old school-mate, and Kitty recognised you. We've – er – helped you already. Remember dantheman? Or journo-jon? They were both really us." Archie stepped closer.

"The tech-queen has already hacked your account so it looks like you've been up to bad stuff.

Most of your 'views' are already illegal. Do you want to leave school with a criminal record?" Kai could smell Archie's disgusting bad breath, and the tang of cigarette smoke on his clothes.

Kitty touched Kai's shoulder. "Do it our way, and all your dreams will come true," she said.

Kai wanted to run for the door. He edged forward.

Archie gripped Kai's arm. "Going somewhere?"

"I just need space to think," said Kai.

He knew he was strong enough to shake Archie off, but it was a risk. Archie might have a knife.

"You don't have time. It's like the tech-queen said... you have to get more than five million 'views' in three days. And you've already wasted one."

Kitty walked round the edge of the table so she was facing Kai. The laptop glow lit her face. Kai saw that her eyes were like Archie's. Fierce. Burning. "Let's get this job finished," she said softly.

Kai wasn't sure if she meant the viral stuff or him – but he wasn't going to wait to find out. Wrenching his arm away from Archie, he dodged round Kitty. Archie grabbed him round the neck, wrestling him in a throat lock. Kai twisted forward. Kitty kicked out at him. A stinging pain shot through his knee. Kai fell. His head hit the corner of the table. He heard a crack of sound then there was a roaring in his ears.

"Think he's passed out," he heard Kitty say.

"Perfect," Archie replied. "We'll give him some time alone. When we come back we'll make him change his mind."

Kai heard the laptop lid snap shut. He heard the tread of footsteps moving away.

He heard the final click of the door being locked.

Chapter Ten
Angry Dragons

Kai tried to stand, but he was dizzy. Smoke stung his eyes and throat. He coughed. A curl of gold licked its way along the edge of the ceiling. The shed was on fire!

He gripped the edge of the table, making himself focus. Flames flickered down the walls like angry dragons.

Kai jumped sideways as burning embers rained onto his neck. It was dark. Smoky. He wasn't sure where the door was. "Help!" He coughed again. "Help! Someone! Anyone!" But there was a band playing inside Street-Level. No one would be outside in the yard. And even if someone saw the shed burning, no one knew he was inside.

Fire ripped along one wall. The ceiling dripped something sticky. The roof was melting. Kai pictured himself melting with it. He pictured flames like dragons, eating his flesh.

He remembered a film at school about burning buildings. You had to stay below the smoke. Victims died of breathing in smoke before the flames got them.

Kai crawled, more sparks spitting into his hair. The second wall was on fire, the wooden planks caving inwards. Soon, the whole building would collapse into a mass of smoke and flames. There was no way he'd find the door in time. "I'm burning up." His voice was a croaked scream. "Help me. Please. PLEASE!"

And then someone was yelling his name. Pulling at him. He was dragged, wrenched, and rolled out through the open door. Everything around him was still burning. He opened his eyes, and saw an angel. Blonde hair. Long, curled eyelashes. A sprinkling of freckles on her soot-smudged nose and cheeks.

Chapter Eleven
Believe in Miracles

"What were you doing in there?" Lena was crying. Matthew Allsop hosed sprays of water at the shed. Someone from the band had sat Kai and Lena in the back of their van.

Kai could hear the screech of sirens further along the street.

"Just, I dunno. Being stupid." Kai's lips hurt and his throat burned, but something stopped him telling the truth. In his fogged brain, he thought if he told on Archie and Kitty, their family might cause trouble for his family. Or they might tell on him. They might tell people about the illegal fake 'likes'. "How did you know I was in there?" he asked Lena in a husky voice.

Lena sniffed. "I didn't. I just came to change my audition song, and when I saw there was a band on I thought I'd hang about by their van. I wanted to get a selfie with them."

The fire sirens screeched louder. Flashing blue lights lit the yard.

"... then I smelled smoke. It was curling up from the shed roof. I was going to run back into Street-Level and get help, but I thought I heard someone calling. I knew there wasn't much time, but it was like a miracle. There was a key in the door."

"So you were going to rescue a stranger?" Kai wasn't sure if he should hug her for being so brave, or yell at her for being so stupid.

"I don't know what I was planning, but when I got the door open, you were just an arm's stretch away. The back of the shed was a wall of flame, but I thought I could reach you. I took a chance."

"Can you tell me your names?" A young woman in a uniform stood looking in at them. "I'm a paramedic. We need to get you both into the ambulance."

Kai looked at Lena. "She took a chance," he thought. All day he'd been angry that Lena had taken his chances away, but she'd taken the only chance that mattered. The chance that had saved his life.

Chapter Twelve
Winners and Losers

Kai left the stage with Lena. They'd just finished their audition duet, 'Sweet Street–Busker'.

"Do you think we were OK?" said Lena. "I thought that girl who sang and played guitar was way better."

Kai shrugged. "I rated that guy who sounded more like Ritchie Ranx than Ritchie Ranx!"

He wasn't bothered about getting through to the final. It had just been a laugh, having a go.

Chelsea came over. "You looked so cool together. I loved the way you took turns and mixed it up," she said.

Sanjay bounced up, waving Kai's phone. "I filmed it all. We can upload it onto the internet back at Lena's."

Kai remembered the horror of the shed. The fire investigators said the blaze had begun with a cigarette-butt tossed onto the roof.

Had Archie done that on purpose? Kai didn't think so – but anyway, Archie had been picked up by the police for some other scam. Dad heard about it in The Crown. Kai wondered if Kitty had been involved. He still remembered the buzz he'd felt when she'd first messaged him. He missed it. Sometimes he hoped she might message him again, but what would she say? And what would he do?

Lena broke into his thoughts. "Maybe we'll go properly viral. Both of us together."

"I'm not up for that again. It's a loser's game," said Kai.

"Pleeeeaaase? Let's at least give it a try," begged Lena.

Kai looked at Lena. Her eyes were full of dreams. He owed her this. "OK," he grinned. "But you three can edit and upload the video. I'll be heading straight for the kebab shop — I'm starving."

Bonus Bits!

Who Said What?

Each of the quotes below comes from one of these people in the story:

1 Lena

2 Kai

3 Sanjay

4 Chelsea

5 Archie Jenkins

Match the person to the quote by writing down the correct letter next to the number on a sheet of paper. Check your answers at the end of this section (no peeking!)

a "Follow your heart."

b "I've got music in my bones."

c "This could be the break I've been dreaming of."

d "... the song sucks."

e "We'll all get rich."

JUDY WAITE

Here are some interesting facts about the author of this book:

- She has won writing awards including 'Best Children's Picture Book'.
- Judy teaches creative writing to university students.
- She has written lots of books for children and young adults.
- She spent some of her childhood in Singapore.
- Judy was born in Portsmouth.
- She has always loved being creative – when she was a child she spent hours in her room writing stories and making comics.

What Next?

Have a think about these questions after reading this story:

- Do you think it was fair for Kai to be cross with Lena when she was upset that he posted the video?
- Do you think Kai and Sanjay should have posted the video online?
- Do you think Kai should have agreed to meet Kitty at all? Why or why not?

Try writing a short guide for other teenagers to show them how to stay safe online so that they don't end up in a situation like Kai's.

ANSWERS to WHO SAID WHAT?

1c, 2b, 3d, 4a, 5e

If you enjoyed reading this story, look out for *Lena's Story: Double Trouble*. Find it, curl up somewhere and READ IT!